THE TROPICAL COOKBOOK

ALIX CAREY

summersdale

THE TROPICAL COOKBOOK

Copyright © Alix Carey, 2020

Marble background © tofutyklein/Shutterstock.com; pineapples © vectornetwork/Shutterstock.com; photos © Alix Carey

An Hachette UK Company
www.hachette.co.uk

Summersdale Publishers Ltd
Part of Octopus Publishing Group Limited
Carmelite House
50 Victoria Embankment
LONDON
EC4Y 0DZ
UK

www.summersdale.com

Printed and bound in the Czech Republic

ISBN: 978-1-78783-284-8

Substantial discounts on bulk quantities of Summersdale books are available to corporations, professional associations and other organizations. For details contact general enquiries: telephone: +44 (0) 1243 771107 or email: enquiries@summersdale.com.

For Nan

ABOUT THE AUTHOR

Alix Carey is a baking enthusiast from Surrey, UK, who combined her passions for baking and writing when she launched her food blog and Instagram account My Kitchen Drawer in 2015.

Carey is a self-confessed dreamer who is also the bestselling author of *The Unicorn Cookbook* (Summersdale, 2017) and *The Mermaid Cookbook* (Summersdale, 2018).

Follow her on Instagram and Twitter **@mykitchendrawer**.

CONTENTS

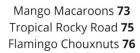

INTRODUCTION

Welcome to *The Tropical Cookbook*, where all your visions of paradise are guaranteed to come true in the form of delicious treats. Inside this vibrant book you'll find 44 fun-filled recipes, ready to help you bring the secrets of the tropics out of the rainforests and into the kitchen. But before you begin Operation Hula, you need to find your Tropicana name. So, what are you waiting for? On the next page, you'll be able to identify your tropical alter ego and begin your baking adventure into the world of the stylish flamingos, cheeky monkeys and playful toucans.

WHAT IS YOUR TROPICANA NAME?

To discover your Tropicana name, find the initial of your first name and the month you were born in the lists below. Combine the two and state your new alias aloud as you don your colourful apron and get ready to hula your way into the kitchen and create a hotter-than-the-tropics feast.

A - COCO
B - EXOTIC
C - ALOHA
D - GLOWING
E - LEI
F - BLOSSOM
G - HULA
H - CALYPSO
I - TIKI
J - RADIANT
K - OCEANIC
L - STORM
M - REEF
N - MANGO
O - SUNRISE
P - TIDE
Q - PARADISE
R - PIÑA
S - BLISS
T - WATERFALL
U - CORAL
V - LOTUS
W - RAINFOREST
X - HURRICANE
Y - SURF
Z - ISLAND

JANUARY - FLAMINGO
FEBRUARY - ORCHID
MARCH - TOUCAN
APRIL - PALM
MAY - TROPICS
JUNE - SAMBA
JULY - HAMMOCK
AUGUST - MONKEY
SEPTEMBER - JELLYFISH
OCTOBER - MONSOON
NOVEMBER - FEATHER
DECEMBER - THUNDER

CONVERSIONS AND MEASUREMENTS

All the conversions in the tables below are close approximates which have been rounded up or down. When using a recipe, always stick to one unit of measurement and do not alternate between them.

LIQUID MEASUREMENTS
5ml = 1 tsp
15ml = 1 tbsp
30ml = ⅛ cup
60ml = ¼ cup
120ml = ½ cup
240ml = 1 cup
2 tbsp liquid egg white = 1 large egg white

BUTTER MEASUREMENTS
30g = ⅛ cup
55g = ¼ cup
75g = ⅓ cup
115g = ½ cup
150g = ⅔ cup
170g = ¾ cup
225g = 1 cup

DRIED INGREDIENT MEASUREMENTS
5g = 1 tsp
15g = 1 tbsp
150g flour = 1 cup
225g caster sugar = 1 cup
115g icing sugar = 1 cup
175g brown sugar = 1 cup
200g sprinkles = 1 cup

OVEN TEMPERATURES

°C	°F	Gas mark
140	275	1
150	300	2
170	325	3
180	350	4
190	375	5
200	400	6
220	425	7
230	450	8
240	475	9

KITCHEN ESSENTIALS

Before we get started, let's take a look at all the essential ingredients and equipment you'll need.

INGREDIENTS

Butter – Unsalted butter is best for baking and it is easiest to use at room temperature, but when you're making pastry it needs to be cold.

Flour – Most of these recipes call for regular plain flour, but occasionally, when baking cakes, I advise using self-raising flour.

Sugar – The most important types of sugar for the recipes in this book are caster sugar, icing sugar and brown sugar.

Fondant icing – Whether it's for coating cakes, topping cupcakes or adorning biscuits, vibrant coloured fondant is a popular ingredient in this book.

Flavour extracts – A number of recipes in this book require vanilla extract, but there are several others that call for more tropical flavourings – such as pineapple, banana, passion fruit and coconut – and these can be found on Amazon or on the website www.foodieflavours.com.

Eggs – Always use large eggs, unless otherwise specified.

Gel food colouring – These are preferred over liquid food colouring because, most importantly, they do not dilute any mixtures and, secondly, you only need to add a few drops to make rich, vibrant colours.

White chocolate – Whether it be for dipping, coating, drizzling or even baking, white chocolate is a big part of many of these recipes. Of course you are welcome to use dark or milk chocolate as a replacement, but white chocolate is used widely as its colour and appearance can be changed easily with food colouring.

Desiccated and flaked coconut – To add that tropical touch to many recipes in this book, it's worth making sure your cupboard is well stocked with these two ingredients.

Dried fruits – You'll want to get your cupboard stocked up with plenty of dried tropical fruit such as papaya, pineapple and mango.

Lemon and lime zest – To help add some fresh flavours to your delicious sweet treats.

Cream cheese – This is used in a couple of recipes in the book. Don't worry if you're dairy-free as you can simply replace dairy cream cheese with soya or other non-dairy options.

EQUIPMENT

Baking trays/tins – You will need at least three flat sheet baking trays, a Swiss roll tin and a 20cm (8in.) square cake tin.

Cake/cupcake tray – All the cakes in this book are baked in round 15cm (6in.) or 20cm (8in.) cake tins and you will need at least two of each (maximum of six). All cupcakes are baked in batches of 12 so you will need a 12-hole cupcake tray.

Baking paper – The majority of recipes will ask you to line a baking tray or cake tin so baking paper is a necessity. *Note: this is not to be confused with greaseproof paper, which is not heat resistant and can cause baked goods to stick to it like glue. Baking paper has a silicone lining and is heat resistant, which prevents any cakes or baked goods from sticking to it.*

Mixing bowls – An assortment of sizes would be ideal, but as long as you have a couple of heatproof mixing bowls you'll get through this book just fine.

Piping bags – Piping bags are used throughout this book for piping buttercream, meringues and batter. You could make your own out of sandwich bags but you'll never achieve the perfectly piped cupcake that way. Piping bags, especially those with a grip, allow you to pipe with absolute accuracy and precision so I would always recommend having a large stash in your kitchen drawer.

Piping nozzles – These come in all shapes and sizes to create a variety of decorations, but I most commonly use the star tips (closed and open), which create decorative swirls, and large round tips for macarons and cake covering.

Palette knife – The palette knife is a great tool for covering your large cakes with icing.

Cookie cutters – You will find these in a huge variety of shapes and sizes, but the main ones you'll need for this book are flower, butterfly, heart, circle and palm-leaf shapes. You can purchase packets of these cutters in every size possible from most high-street kitchen retailers.

Rolling pin – A kitchen necessity for bashing biscuits (for a cheesecake base) as well as rolling out pastry and fondant.

Cupcake cases – When making cupcakes, you'll need cupcake cases and you can be as adventurous as you wish with the colours. Vibrant colours are the perfect choice for these recipes.

Electric whisk or standing mixer – While I advocate the use of your own strength, you'll find an electric whisk or standing mixer much easier and quicker for many of these recipes.

Scales – Baking is a science and requires the precise measurement of ingredients.

Measuring spoons – My baking besties. A little lesson to remember: a teaspoon is 5ml and a tablespoon is 15ml. Avoid using normal cutlery to approximate these, as spoons can range between 2ml and 10ml. This might not sound like much difference, but a sponge cake can crack or sink on as little as a few grams too much or too little baking powder.

Cake tester – Some of us can tell when a cake is cooked just by looking at it, but to save yourself from that dreaded sunken uncooked sponge it's best to get yourself a cake tester so you can check if it's cooked all the way through.

Icing smoother – The perfect tool for creating that perfectly smooth buttercream on all your celebration cakes.

Fondant smoother – Like the icing smoother, this is the perfect tool for smoothing the fondant over and around your celebration cakes and removing air bubbles.

Decorating turntable – A 360° rotating table makes icing cakes a doddle and allows for easy piping, smoothing and decorating.

CUPCAKES

🍍 FLAMIA THE FLAMINGO CUPCAKES 🍍

She's pretty, pink and perfectly edible. Please give a warm welcome to Flamia the Flamingo! She'll be making an appearance throughout the book, but this time round she's here to steal the show with her delicious cupcakes.

Makes: 12 🍍 Time: 2 hours 🍍 Difficulty rating: 🦩🦩

INGREDIENTS

For the vanilla cupcakes:

- 150g butter, softened
- 150g caster sugar
- 3 eggs
- 150g self-raising flour
- ¼ tsp vanilla extract
- Pink gel food colouring

For the buttercream:

- 200g butter, softened
- 400g icing sugar
- Pink gel food colouring

EXTRA EQUIPMENT

You will need a 12-hole cupcake tray, 12 cupcake cases, a piping bag and a closed-star piping nozzle.

METHOD

For the vanilla cupcakes:

Preheat the oven to 180°C and line a cupcake tray with 12 cupcake cases.

Put the butter, sugar, eggs and flour in a large mixing bowl, and beat together until pale and fluffy. Add the vanilla extract and two drops of pink gel food colouring then mix through until well combined.

Fill each cupcake case with a heaped tablespoon of batter, then bake in the oven for 20–25 minutes until springy to touch. Remove the tray from the oven and place the cupcakes on a wire rack to cool.

For the buttercream:

Blend the butter and icing sugar together until smooth, add a few drops of pink gel food colouring (enough to make the buttercream a tropical pink colour) and combine.

Fit a piping bag with a closed-star nozzle, transfer the mixture into the piping bag and pipe swirls of buttercream on top of the cupcakes.

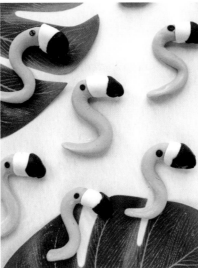

To decorate, insert a fondant flamingo head and two fondant flamingo wings (see the next recipe) into the buttercream. The fondant head can be inserted into one side of the cupcake facing out, followed by two heart-shaped wings either side (one on the left and one on the right).

These will last for 2–3 days in an airtight container kept somewhere cool.

FONDANT FLAMINGO DECORATIONS

Bring Flamia to life with these easy-to-make fondant flamingo heads and wings.

Makes: 12   Time: 1 hour (plus overnight drying time)

Difficulty rating:

INGREDIENTS

- 250g pink fondant icing
- 100g white fondant icing
- 100g black fondant icing

EXTRA EQUIPMENT

You will need a rolling pin, a small, clean cake-decorating paintbrush, a cocktail stick and a 2cm (1in.) heart-shaped cutter.

METHOD

For the flamingo heads:

Using 150g of pink fondant, take 12 small marble-sized balls and roll them into sausage shapes so that one end is thicker than the other. Mould them into "S" shapes with the thicker end at the top.

Take 12 smaller balls of white fondant icing and roll them out into rectangles.

Brush the white fondant rectangles with a damp paintbrush then wrap the white fondant around the thicker end of the pink fondant and press down lightly with your finger around where the two fondants meet so they fuse together. Leave to one side.

With the black fondant, take 12 pea-sized balls and roll them out into rectangles. Brush them with a damp paintbrush then wrap the black fondant around the end of the white fondant and press down lightly with your finger where the two fondants meet so they fuse together. This is your flamingo beak.

Using a cocktail stick, poke a hole to the left of the beak then take a tiny piece of black fondant and poke it inside for the eye.

Leave the flamingo heads out at room temperature on a lined baking tray to dry overnight. These will keep at room temperature for 2–3 days in an airtight container.

For the flamingo wings:

Using the remaining 100g pink fondant, roll it out to the thickness of 3mm. Using the 2cm (1in.) heart cutter, cut out as many hearts as you can and put them on to a lined baking tray. Re-roll the pink fondant and continue cutting out hearts until you have 24 in total.

Leave them on the lined baking tray at room temperature to dry overnight. These will keep at room temperature for 2–3 days in an airtight container.

🍍 TROPICAL ISLAND CUPCAKES 🍍

If you were stranded on a desert island, these cupcakes would definitely be on your must-have list.

Serves: 12 🍍 Time: 2 hours 🍍 Difficulty rating: 🦩🦩

INGREDIENTS

For the coconut cupcakes:

* 150g butter, softened
* 150g caster sugar
* 3 eggs
* 150g self-raising flour
* ¼ tsp vanilla extract
* 50g desiccated coconut

For the pineapple buttercream:

* 100g desiccated coconut
* 200g butter, softened
* 400g icing sugar
* 2–3 drops pineapple flavouring

For the palm-tree sticks:

* 4 sesame breadsticks
* 200g white chocolate
* 1–2 drops green gel food colouring
* Green sprinkles

EXTRA EQUIPMENT

You will need a 12-hole cupcake tray, 12 cupcake cases (preferably a mixture of green and blue), a piping bag and a round-tip piping nozzle. For the palm trees, you will need a flat baking tray and a piping bag.

METHOD

For the coconut cupcakes:

Preheat the oven to 180°C and line a cupcake tray with 12 cupcake cases.

Add the butter, sugar, eggs and flour in a large mixing bowl, and beat together until pale and fluffy. Add the vanilla extract and desiccated coconut and mix through until well combined.

Fill each cupcake case with a heaped tablespoon of batter and bake in the oven for 20–25 minutes until the sponge is just browned and springy to touch. Leave to cool on a wire rack and leave the oven on, keeping to 180°C.

For the pineapple buttercream:

Firstly, spread out the desiccated coconut on a baking tray and put into the oven to toast, checking every few minutes and stirring it around so all pieces get toasted. Once lightly browned, remove from the oven and leave to cool slightly while you make the buttercream.

Place the softened butter and icing sugar in a large bowl and beat together until smooth and fluffy. Add the pineapple flavouring and

combine. Then fit a piping bag with a round-tip piping nozzle and fill the bag with the buttercream.

Pour the toasted coconut into a bowl then pipe mounds of buttercream on to the cupcakes and dip the tops into the toasted coconut before topping with a palm-tree stick.

For the palm-tree sticks:

Line a flat baking tray with baking paper and set aside.

Cut four sesame breadsticks into three lengths to make 12 shorter sticks and lay them out on the baking tray in two rows.

Break the chocolate into a medium bowl and set it over a pan of simmering water. Stir occasionally until the chocolate has melted then add a few drops of green gel food colouring and stir it through.

Remove the bowl from the heat and let the chocolate cool to room temperature before pouring it into a piping bag.

Snip the end of the piping bag then pipe your spiky palm leaves on top of the sesame breadsticks and top with green sprinkles. Leave them to set in the fridge for 30 minutes before carefully peeling away from the baking paper. Stick them into the cupcakes to create mini tropical islands, and if you make more you can always eat them on their own.

🍍 WATERMELON CUPCAKES 🍍

Mouth-wateringly delicious, these cupcakes are the perfect afternoon treat.

Makes: 12 🍍 Time: 2 hours 🍍 Difficulty rating: 🦩🦩

INGREDIENTS

For the vanilla cupcakes:

* 150g butter, softened
* 150g caster sugar
* 3 eggs
* 150g self-raising flour
* ¼ tsp vanilla extract
* Green gel food colouring

For the buttercream:

* 200g butter, softened
* 400g icing sugar
* Pink gel food colouring
* Chocolate chips, to decorate

EXTRA EQUIPMENT

You will need a 12-hole cupcake tray, 12 cupcake cases, a piping bag and a closed-star piping nozzle.

METHOD

For the vanilla cupcakes:

Preheat the oven to 180°C and line a cupcake tray with 12 cupcake cases.

Put the butter, sugar, eggs and flour in a large mixing bowl, and beat together until pale and fluffy. Add the vanilla extract and two drops of green gel food colouring then mix through until well combined.

Fill each cupcake case with a heaped tablespoon of batter, then bake in the oven for 20–25 minutes until springy to touch. Remove the tray from the oven and place the cupcakes on a wire rack to cool.

For the buttercream:

Blend the butter and icing sugar together until smooth, add a few drops of the pink gel food colouring (enough to make the buttercream a vibrant pink hue) and combine.

Fit a piping bag with a closed-star nozzle, transfer the mixture into the piping bag and pipe swirls of buttercream on top of the cupcakes.

To decorate, scatter some chocolate chips on to the buttercream, spacing them apart to resemble watermelon seeds.

These will last for 2–3 days in an airtight container kept somewhere cool.

🍍 PALM LEAF CUPCAKES 🍍

Take your tropical-themed party to the next level
with these stylish, sumptuous sweet treats.

Makes: 12 cupcakes 🍍 Time: 2 hours 🍍 Difficulty rating: 🦩🦩

INGREDIENTS

For the orange cupcakes:

- 150g butter, softened
- 150g caster sugar
- 3 eggs
- 150g self-raising flour
- Zest of 1 orange
- ¼ tsp vanilla extract

For the fondant leaves:

- 200g green fondant icing

For the vanilla buttercream:

- 200g butter, softened
- 400g icing sugar, plus extra for dusting
- 1 tbsp vanilla extract
- Pink gel food colouring

EXTRA EQUIPMENT

You will need a 12-hole cupcake tray, 12 cupcake cases (preferably green and orange), a piping bag, a round-tip piping nozzle, a tropical leaf cookie cutter (in this recipe, I've used a monstera leaf cutter) and a rolling pin.

METHOD

For the orange cupcakes:

Preheat the oven to 180°C and line a cupcake tray with 12 cupcake cases.

Add the butter, sugar, eggs, flour and orange zest in a large mixing bowl, and beat together until pale and fluffy. Add the vanilla extract and mix through until well combined.

Fill each cupcake case with a tablespoon of batter and bake in the oven for 20–25 minutes until the sponge is just browned and springy to touch. Leave to cool on a wire rack.

For the fondant leaves:

Dust a hard surface with icing sugar then roll out the green fondant until it's 2.5mm thick.

Dip your tropical leaf cutter into a bowl of icing sugar (to help stop the icing sticking to the cutter) then cut out 12 leaves, taking the time to carefully poke out any excess that hasn't cut out fully (i.e. the holes in the centre).

Dust off any excess icing sugar from the leaves then pop the leaves on a baking tray somewhere cool and dry for 30 minutes to dry out and harden a little while you make the buttercream.

For the vanilla buttercream:

Place the softened butter and icing sugar in a large bowl and beat together until smooth and fluffy. Add the vanilla extract and a tiny drop of pink food colouring then combine. (You want to be really sparing with the food colouring in order to create a peach tone.)

Fit a piping bag with the round-tip piping nozzle then fill it with the pink buttercream and pipe a mound of buttercream on top of each cupcake.

Top each one with a tropical leaf and serve.

These will keep in the fridge in an airtight container for 2–3 days.

🍍 HULA-HULA CUPCAKES 🍍

Dig out that flowery garland and hula your way into the kitchen to make these cupcakes that'll give your guests a spring in their step (or a hula in their hop).

Makes: 12 cupcakes 🍍 Time: 2 hours 🍍 Difficulty rating: 🦩🦩

INGREDIENTS

For the chocolate orange cupcakes:

- 150g butter, softened
- 150g caster sugar
- 3 eggs
- 150g self-raising flour
- Zest of 1 orange
- 50g cocoa powder
- ¼ tsp vanilla extract

For the vanilla buttercream:

- 400g icing sugar
- 200g butter, softened
- 1 tbsp vanilla extract
- Blue, green, orange and red gel food colouring

EXTRA EQUIPMENT

You will need a 12-hole cupcake tray, 12 cupcake cases, 4 small piping bags, a large closed-star, a small closed-star, a large open-star and a small petal-tip piping nozzle.

METHOD

For the chocolate orange cupcakes:

Preheat the oven to 180°C and line a cupcake tray with 12 cupcake cases.

Add the butter, sugar, eggs, flour, orange zest and cocoa powder in a large mixing bowl, and beat together until pale and fluffy. Add the vanilla extract and mix through until well combined.

Fill each cupcake case with a heaped tablespoon of batter and bake in the oven for 20–25 minutes until the sponge is just browned and springy to touch. Leave to cool on a wire rack.

For the vanilla buttercream:

Place the icing sugar and softened butter in a large bowl and beat together until smooth and fluffy. Add the vanilla extract and combine then split the mixture equally between four bowls.

Add a few drops of blue food colouring to one of the bowls and mix it through, adding more if you wish, until you have a bright blue colour. Add a different colour food colouring to each bowl, until you have one bowl of each colour.

Fit four piping bags with your piping nozzles, then transfer the blue buttercream to the piping bag fitted with the petal-tip nozzle, the green buttercream to the piping bag fitted with the open-star nozzle, the orange buttercream to the piping bag fitted with the large closed-star nozzle and the red buttercream to the piping bag fitted with the small closed-star nozzle.

Starting with the green buttercream, pipe a small amount on to one part of each cupcake, then move to the blue buttercream and pipe in another section, followed by the orange buttercream and finally the red. Fill in any gaps as you wish, using any piping tip, until you have covered the cupcakes to resemble the flowers on a lei garland.

CELEBRATION CAKES

 FABULOUS FEATHER CAKE

*Giving flamingos a run for their money, this fabulous feather
cake is a showstopper to behold.*

Serves: 12 ● Time: 3 hours ● Difficulty rating: 🦩🦩🦩

INGREDIENTS

For the raspberry cake:

* 250g butter, softened
* 250g caster sugar
* 6 eggs
* 1 tsp vanilla extract
* 1–2 drops raspberry flavouring
* 200g self-raising flour
* ½ tsp baking powder

For the raspberry buttercream:

* 500g butter, softened
* 900g icing sugar
* 1 tsp vanilla extract
* 1–2 drops raspberry flavouring

For the chocolate feathers:

* 200g white chocolate
* Pink gel food colouring

EXTRA EQUIPMENT

You will need two 15cm wide x 7cm deep (6in. wide x 3in. deep) cake tins, a 15cm diameter (6in. diameter) cake board, a palette knife, an icing smoother, a decorating turntable and a wide, clean decorating paintbrush.

METHOD

For the raspberry cake:

Preheat the oven to 180°C and line the two 15cm (6in.) cake tins with baking paper.

Place the butter in a large saucepan set over a low heat until it has melted, but don't let it boil. Add the sugar and stir to create a paste, then add the eggs one by one, mixing well in between.

Add the vanilla extract and raspberry flavouring and fold in the flour and baking powder until well combined.

Divide the cake batter between the two lined cake tins and bake for 30–40 minutes until browned and springy to touch.

Remove from the oven and leave to cool in the tins for 15 minutes before lifting out and placing on a wire rack to cool completely. Once cool, cut the two sponge cakes in half so you have four layers ready for assembling.

For the raspberry buttercream:

Put the butter in a bowl and beat until smooth, then slowly sift in the icing sugar. Stir through the vanilla extract and raspberry flavouring and continue mixing until smooth.

For the chocolate feathers:

Line two baking trays with baking paper and set aside.

Break the white chocolate into small pieces, place them in a heatproof bowl over a pan of simmering water and, stirring occasionally, let the chocolate melt down completely.

Split the melted chocolate equally into four small bowls and colour each bowl with pink gel food colouring. Start with one drop in one bowl, two drops in the second, followed by three in the third and four drops in the fourth bowl, stirring them all until the colour is well mixed.

Using a tablespoon, spoon blobs of chocolate, one colour at a time, on to the lined baking tray. Then take a clean wide paintbrush and brush through to drag out the chocolate into long feather shapes.

Repeat with the other colours, washing the spoon and brushing thoroughly in between, then leave the chocolate feathers to set in the fridge for 1 hour. You need approximately 20–25 feathers for the cake, but make more as these are very fragile when they have set.

Assembling the cake:

Add a little buttercream to the 15cm (6in.) cake board so that your first sponge layer can be secured to the base. Continue sandwiching the remaining sponge layers with a generous portion of the chocolate buttercream in between each layer.

Cover the entire cake with a thin layer of the buttercream and smooth it out with a palette knife, then leave in the fridge for an hour to harden.

Add a second, thicker coat of the buttercream, then use a palette knife to smooth it out.

Place the cake on the decorating turntable. Take your icing smoother, holding it lightly on the cake with the bottom touching the turntable, and rotate the cake. If you need to go around the cake again, clean your icing smoother and repeat.

Remove the chocolate feathers from the baking paper carefully by peeling the paper away from the feather rather than the other way around.

Working from the top downward, fix the feathers to your cake using a little buttercream as glue to bind, mixing up the shades of pink and the different sizes and overlapping them occasionally.

Eat quickly before she flocks away or keep for up to 2–3 days at room temperature in an airtight container.

🍍 PINEAPPLE POWER CAKE 🍍

Revel in your guests' wonder as they marvel at the beautiful icing intricacies of this zesty, extravagant celebration cake.

Serves: 10–12 🍍 Time: 2–3 hours 🍍 Difficulty rating: 🦩🦩🦩

INGREDIENTS

For the pineapple cake:

- 300g butter, softened
- 300g caster sugar
- 300g self-raising flour
- 1 tsp baking powder
- 4 eggs
- 1 tsp vanilla extract
- 2–3 drops pineapple flavouring

For the pineapple buttercream:

- 500g butter, softened
- 1kg icing sugar
- Pineapple flavouring
- Yellow and green gel food colouring

For the pineapple leaves:

- 100g white chocolate
- Green gel food colouring

EXTRA EQUIPMENT

You will need two 15cm wide x 7cm deep (6in. wide x 3in. deep) cake tins, baking paper, a 20cm (8in.) cake board, a palette knife, an icing smoother, a decorating turntable, a piping bag, a 2cm (1in.) closed-star nozzle and a clean 3cm-thick (1⅛in.-thick) baking paintbrush.

METHOD

For the pineapple cake:

Preheat the oven to 180ºC and prepare two 15cm (6in.) cake tins with baking paper.

Add the butter, sugar, flour, baking powder and eggs into a bowl and whisk together for 2–3 minutes until smooth, pale and fluffy. Add the vanilla extract and pineapple flavouring and mix through, then fill the cake tins evenly with the batter.

Bake for 25 minutes until golden and springy to touch.

Remove from the oven and leave to cool in the tins before turning them out on to a wire rack to cool completely.

For the pineapple buttercream:

Combine the butter and icing sugar in a large bowl, and whisk with a standing mixer or handheld electric whisk for 4 minutes until smooth, pale and fluffy.

Scoop a quarter of the buttercream into a bowl, then cover it and leave to one side until later. Add two to three drops of pineapple flavouring and yellow food colouring to the rest of the buttercream then mix it through until it's a bright yellow colour.

For the pineapple leaves:

Put the white chocolate into a heatproof bowl and set it over a pan of simmering water to melt.

Once melted, add a few drops of green food colouring and stir it though, adding more colouring until you get the green leaf colour you desire.

Line a baking tray with baking paper then spoon out a tablespoon of the white chocolate. Using a wide baking paintbrush, gently brush through the chocolate to give a paintbrush effect.

Continue a few more times, creating different lengths, then leave in the freezer to set hard for at least 30 minutes.

Assembling the cake:

Cut the two layers of cake in half so you have four layers of sponge, then add a little yellow buttercream to a 20cm (8in.) cake board and place one of the sponge layers on top. Continue sandwiching the remaining sponge layers one by one on top with a generous portion of yellow buttercream in between each layer.

Set aside a bowl with half of the yellow buttercream to be used later. Then cover the entire cake with a thin layer of some of the remaining buttercream, smooth it out with a palette knife and then leave in the fridge for an hour so the butter hardens.

Add a second, thicker coat of the yellow buttercream then use a palette knife to smooth it out. Place the cake on the decorating turntable. Take your icing smoother, holding it lightly on the cake with the bottom touching the turntable, and rotate the cake. If you need to go around the cake again, clean your icing smoother and repeat.

Take the bowl of plain buttercream and colour it with a few drops of green food colouring and a drop of yellow until you have a kiwi-green colour.

Fit a piping bag with a 2cm (1in.) closed-star piping nozzle then fill the piping bag with the remaining yellow buttercream on one side and the green buttercream on the other. This will give you a two-tone buttercream when it's piped.

Starting from the bottom, pipe little stars of buttercream around the cake, continuing around the cake until you get to the top, then continue piping over the top of the cake.

When you are ready to serve the cake, stick the white-chocolate pineapple leaves into the top of it and serve immediately.

The cake will keep for 2–3 days in an airtight container.

RAINFOREST CAKE

It's been a hot day at the beach, but it's time to cool down under the canopy with a slice of this light and fluffy cake.

Serves: 10–12   Time: 2–3 hours   Difficulty rating: 🦩🦩🦩

INGREDIENTS

For the vanilla cake:

* 300g butter, softened
* 300g caster sugar
* 300g self-raising flour
* 1 tsp baking powder
* 4 eggs
* 1 tsp vanilla extract

For the buttercream:

* 250g butter, softened
* 500g icing sugar

For the tropical leaves and icing:

* Icing sugar, for dusting
* 200g green fondant
* 600g white fondant
* 2 A4 sheets of palm-print icing paper

EXTRA EQUIPMENT

You will need two 15cm wide x 7cm deep (6in. wide x 3in. deep) cake tins, a 20cm (8in.) cake board, a palette knife, an icing smoother, a decorating turntable, a tropical leaf cutter, a fondant smoother, a ruler, a pencil, scissors, a baking paintbrush and a rolling pin.

METHOD

For the vanilla cake:

Preheat the oven to 180°C and prepare the two cake tins with baking paper.

Add the butter, sugar, flour, baking powder, eggs and vanilla extract into a bowl and whisk together for 2–3 minutes until smooth, pale and fluffy, then fill the cake tins evenly with the batter.

Bake for 25 minutes until golden and a cake tester comes out clean.

Remove from the oven and leave to cool in the tins before shortly turning them out on to a wire rack to cool completely.

For the buttercream:

Place the butter and icing sugar in a large bowl and whisk with a standing mixer or handheld whisk for 4 minutes until smooth, pale and fluffy.

For the tropical leaves:

Dust a hard surface with a little icing sugar and roll out the green fondant to a 1cm thickness.

Dip the tropical leaf cutter in a little icing sugar then cut out 5–6 leaves.

Put the leaves to one side while you assemble the cake.

Assembling the cake:

Cut the cakes in half horizontally so you have three layers of sponge, then add a little buttercream to the 20cm (8in.) cake board and place one of the sponge layers on top. Continue sandwiching the remaining sponge layers one by one with a generous portion of buttercream in between each layer.

Sit the cake on top of an icing turntable then cover the entire cake with a thin layer of buttercream and smooth it out with a palette knife, then leave in the fridge for an hour for the buttercream to harden.

Add a second, thicker coat of buttercream, using a palette knife to smooth it around, then take your icing smoother and place it lightly on the cake, with the bottom touching the turntable, and rotate the cake. If you need to go around the cake again, clean your icing smoother and repeat. Put the cake to one side.

Dust the kitchen surface with a little icing sugar and roll out the white fondant to 45cm (18in.) in diameter. (For cakes of other sizes, the formula to work out how much fondant to use is: cake diameter + height x 2.)

Shape the fondant into a ball and roll from the centre out, lifting and spinning the fondant around to avoid it sticking and so you can roll it out into an even circle. Keep rolling until you have a 45cm diameter (18in. diameter) circle that is around 1.8cm thick.

To place over the cake, gently lift the white fondant over the rolling pin and position the fondant centrally over the sponge. Carefully smooth it down around the sides using a fondant smoother. Trim off the excess fondant using a sharp knife, then smooth the edges down.

Next, measure and cut out the A4 palm-print icing paper so that it is the same height as the cake (approximately 15cm [6in.]). Using a clean baking paintbrush, dab the white fondant with a little cold water all around the edges. Then peel away the baking paper and carefully stick the printed icing paper to the side of the cake, smoothing it out with your hands.

Decorate the top with your green fondant palm leaves and serve.

The cake will keep for 2–3 days in an airtight container.

🍍 "IT'S BANANAS" CAKE 🍍

It's time to make your guests go bananas for a cake that is big, bold and bonkers.
But first, you must make it...

Serves: 10–12 🍍 Time: 2–3 hours 🍍 Difficulty rating: 🦩🦩🦩

INGREDIENTS

For the banana cake:

* 3 large ripe bananas
* 2 tsp vanilla extract
* 300g self-raising flour
* 1 tsp baking powder
* ½ tsp salt
* 1 tsp cinnamon
* 200g butter, softened
* 300g light brown sugar
* 3 eggs
* 100ml semi-skimmed milk

For the banana buttercream:

* 400g butter, softened
* 800g icing sugar
* 2–3 drops yellow gel food colouring
* 2–3 drops banana flavouring

For the chocolate sails:

* 100g milk chocolate

For the chocolate drip:

* 100g dark chocolate

For the decorations:

* 3 drops banana flavouring
* Foam bananas
* Banana chips
* Flaked chocolate

EXTRA EQUIPMENT

You will need two 15cm wide x 7cm deep (6in. wide x 3in. deep) cake tins, baking paper, a flat baking tray, a 20cm (8in.) cake board, a palette knife, an icing smoother, a decorating turntable, a piping bag, a round-tip icing nozzle and pegs.

METHOD

For the banana cake:

Preheat the oven to 180°C and prepare the two round cake tins with baking paper.

Peel and mash the bananas in a large bowl, then add the vanilla extract and mix it through. Set aside.

In another large bowl, mix together the flour, baking powder, salt and cinnamon, then set aside.

In a third large bowl, cream together the butter and light brown sugar until pale and fluffy, then add the eggs one by one, beating well in between each one. Sift in half the flour mixture then mix well.

Slowly add in the milk and then fold in the remaining flour followed by the mashed banana.

Tip the mixture into the prepared tins and level the top.

Place in the oven and bake for about one hour, until the cake is golden brown and a cake tester comes out clean. If the sponge begins to get too brown, cover the top with some tinfoil to stop it burning.

Remove from the oven and leave to cool in the tins before shortly turning out on to a wire rack to cool completely.

For the banana buttercream:

Combine the butter and icing sugar in a large mixing bowl until smooth, pale and fluffy, then mix in the yellow food colouring and banana flavouring until you create a bright yellow colour.

For the chocolate sails:

To make the chocolate sail topper, prepare a flat baking tray with two separate pieces of baking paper, then break the milk chocolate into a bowl and set it over a pan of simmering water to melt.

Once the chocolate has melted, drizzle two tablespoons of the chocolate on to one of the pieces of baking paper and spread it out into a thin circle. To create the sail shape, take one end of the baking paper then pinch the corners together and clip securely with a peg.

Repeat with the other piece of baking paper then put the baking tray in the fridge for the chocolate to set.

Assembling the cake:

Remove the banana cakes from the tins and cut each in half horizontally so you have four layers. Add a little buttercream to the 20cm (8in.) cake board and secure one of the cake layers to it.

Fill a piping bag with buttercream, cut the end, then pipe the buttercream on to the top of the sponge layer and spread it out across the entire surface. Add the next layer of sponge and repeat the process with the other sponges.

Sit the cake on top of an icing turntable then cover the entire cake with a thin layer of buttercream and smooth it out with a palette knife and an icing smoother.

Leave in the fridge for an hour until the buttercream has hardened.

For the chocolate drip:

Break the dark chocolate into pieces and place it in a heatproof bowl set over a pan of simmering water to melt gently.

Take the cake out of the fridge and place it back on to the turntable. Using a tablespoon, spoon the melted chocolate on to the centre of the cake. Then, using the back of the spoon, spread the chocolate around until the top of the cake is completely covered and enough of the liquid chocolate reaches the edges.

Slowly push a bit of the chocolate over the edge with the back of the spoon so it drips down the sides and continue to do this all the way around. It looks nicer when drips aren't uniform so you can push a bit more and a bit less as you go along.

For the decorations:

Remove the chocolate sails from the fridge and carefully peel the baking paper away.

Make a small incision into the top of the cake where you want the sails to sit, then poke them into the incision.

Finish decorating the rest of the cake with foam bananas, banana chips and flaked chocolate, then serve.

This will keep, stored airtight and somewhere cool, for 2–3 days.

🍍 COCONUT CAKE 🍍

Savour the tropical tastes of this creamy cake,
which at first your guests may mistake for a real coconut!

Serves: 10–12 🍍 Time: 2–3 hours 🍍 Difficulty rating: 🦩🦩

INGREDIENTS

For the coconut cake:

* 500g butter, softened, plus extra for greasing
* 500g caster sugar
* 500g self-raising flour
* 2 tsp baking powder
* 6 eggs
* 1 tsp vanilla extract
* 100g desiccated coconut

For the chocolate coating:

* 500g dark chocolate

For the chocolate buttercream:

* 250g butter, softened
* 500g icing sugar
* 50g cocoa powder
* 2 tsp vanilla extract

EXTRA EQUIPMENT

You will need two 20cm (8in.) half-sphere cake tins, a palette knife, two large baking trays, baking paper, a piping bag, a writing-tip nozzle, an icing smoother, a 20cm (8in.) cake board, a 6cm (2½in.) circle cookie cutter and a decorating turntable.

METHOD

For the coconut cake:

Preheat the oven to 180°C and prepare two half-sphere cake tins by greasing with butter.

Add the butter, sugar, flour, baking powder, eggs and vanilla extract into a bowl and whisk together for 2–3 minutes until smooth, pale and fluffy, then add the desiccated coconut and fold it all together.

Split the batter evenly between the two cake tins then bake for 45 minutes–1 hour, until golden and a cake tester comes out clean. *Tip: create a nest with tinfoil for the cake tins to sit in while they bake so they don't roll in the oven.*

Leave the sponges to cool a little in the tins then, shortly later, turn them out on to a wire rack to cool completely.

For the chocolate coating:

Break the chocolate into a heatproof bowl set over a pan of simmering water. Leave the chocolate to melt, stirring occasionally until completely melted.

Remove the bowl from the heat and leave the chocolate to cool to room temperature. Meanwhile, line two baking trays with baking paper.

Fit a piping bag with a writing-tip nozzle then pour the cooled chocolate into a piping bag.

Carefully pipe approximately 20cm (8in.) lines on to both the prepared baking sheets until fully covered, then leave in the fridge to set for 30 minutes.

Once set, remove the baking sheets from the fridge and, using an icing smoother or another flat utensil, push it against the chocolate to lift the set lines off the baking paper so you have lots of little chocolate strips.

Continue piping and setting more chocolate until you have used all the chocolate, then leave the chocolate strips in the fridge to keep hard while you make the buttercream.

For the chocolate buttercream:

Combine the butter and icing sugar in a large bowl and whisk with a standing mixer or handheld whisk for 4 minutes until smooth, pale and fluffy.

Take out a few tablespoons of the white mixture and leave to one side for later.

With the remaining mixture, add the cocoa powder and vanilla extract and fold it through until fully combined, then leave to one side while you prepare the cake.

Level out the flat sides of both sponges with a sharp knife then slice off the top of one half's rounded section and place it small side down on the cake board with a little buttercream to secure it.

Spread out some more buttercream on the top of the sponge then place the other sponge layer on top to create a sphere shape.

To make it look like a coconut drink, cut about 6cm (2½in.) off the top of the sphere using a 6cm (2½in.) circle cookie cutter, then smooth out the small hole using a tablespoon.

Place the cake on to the decorating turntable and coat it in a thin layer of buttercream, using a palette knife to smooth it all out. Put the cake in the fridge for 30 minutes before coating it again with another layer of buttercream. Make sure your hollowed-out section has a nice thick coating of the white buttercream you saved earlier.

Place the cake on to a wire rack, then begin carefully sticking chocolate strips to the sides of the cake. Leave the hollowed-out section clear. Continue around the entire cake until all sides are fully coated with chocolate to resemble the coconut shell.

To decorate, add a fancy straw, a cocktail stirrer and a cocktail umbrella and you're ready to serve your own edible paradise drink.

The cake will keep for 2–3 days in an airtight container.

COOKIES AND BISCUITS

🍍 PINEAPPLE MACARONS 🍍

Let the silky, light texture and zesty kick of these pineapple macarons transport you to an exotic paradise you won't ever forget.

Makes: 12 🍍 Time: 2 hours 🍍 Difficulty rating: 🦩🦩🦩

INGREDIENTS

For the macaron shells:

* 70g ground almonds
* 140g icing sugar
* 2 egg whites, at room temperature
* Yellow gel food colouring
* 50g caster sugar
* 100g white chocolate
* Green gel food colouring

For the pineapple curd filling:

* 150g caster sugar
* 100ml pineapple juice
* 2 eggs
* 2 egg yolks
* 2 tbsp cornflour
* 85g butter, cubed

EXTRA EQUIPMENT

You will need a standing mixer or handheld electric whisk, two baking trays, a piping bag and a small round-tip piping nozzle. To decorate, you will need two piping bags and a writing-tip nozzle.

METHOD

For the macaron shells:

Preheat the oven to 140–150°C, line two baking trays with baking paper and set aside.

Place the ground almonds and icing sugar in a standing mixer or use a handheld electric whisk and blitz for about a minute, then transfer to a mixing bowl.

Beat one of the egg whites into the almond and icing sugar mixture to make a smooth paste. Add a few drops of yellow gel food colouring and mix to combine fully, then cover the bowl with a tea towel.

Pour the second egg white into a super-clean bowl and begin to whisk on high speed to form peaks. Gradually add the caster sugar 1 tablespoon at a time, until it starts to stiffen. Once all the sugar has been added, continue beating on a high setting for 2 minutes until the mixture resembles stiff, glossy peaks.

Add the egg-white mixture to the almond paste and, using a spatula, fold the two together from the bottom up. Continue that motion around 15–20 times until the mixture is fully incorporated and flows like molten lava.

49

Transfer the mixture into a piping bag fitted with a small round-tip nozzle and pipe 24 small rounds on to the two lined baking trays. The mixture will spread so pipe to around 50 per cent of the size you want.

Tap the trays on a work surface a few times to release any air bubbles, then leave them to dry for 30 minutes. They will be ready to bake when they are no longer sticky or wet when touched.

Bake on the middle shelf of the oven for 8 minutes. Open the oven to let out any steam and turn the trays around, then bake for a further 8 minutes until the tops are crisp.

Remove from the oven and leave them to cool fully before removing from the baking sheet.

To decorate the shells, melt the white chocolate by breaking it into small pieces and placing it in a heatproof bowl over a pan of simmering water. Stir occasionally until the chocolate has melted down completely then take off the heat to cool down to room temperature.

Fit a piping bag with a writing-tip nozzle and fill it with the melted white chocolate (leave a small amount in the bowl for the pineapple leaves) then pipe criss-crosses across half of the shells to resemble pineapple skin.

Colour the leftover white chocolate with a couple of drops of green gel food colouring. Using a clean piping bag and the writing-tip nozzle, pipe out 36 small pineapple leaves (three per macaron) on to some baking paper and set them aside in the fridge to harden.

For the pineapple curd filling:

In a medium saucepan whisk the sugar, pineapple juice, eggs, egg yolks and cornflour together until smooth. Place over a low heat and stir continuously until the ingredients are melted and fully combined.

Add the butter 3–4 cubes at a time, stirring until each has melted before adding more.

Continue stirring for around 6 more minutes or until the curd is thick enough to coat the back of a spoon.

Pour into a bowl and leave to cool.

Once cool, spread a teaspoon of pineapple curd on to the plain macaron shells and then top with the decorated ones.

Stick the pineapple leaves in between the macaron shells.

Leave in the fridge for 30 minutes before serving.

These will store in an airtight container for a few days if kept in the fridge.

HIBISCUS BISCUITS

Associated with everything tropical, the hibiscus is even the state flower of Hawaii. Create your own edible sort with these vibrant, melt-in-the-mouth biscuits.

Makes: 12   Time: 2 hours   Difficulty rating:

INGREDIENTS

For the orange biscuits:

- 85g unsalted butter
- 100g golden caster sugar
- 1 egg
- ½ tsp vanilla extract
- Zest of 1 orange
- 200g plain flour, plus extra for dusting
- ¼ tsp salt
- ½ tsp baking powder

For the icing decorations:

- 100g orange modelling fondant
- 100g purple modelling fondant
- 100g hot-pink modelling fondant
- 150g white modelling fondant
- 50g yellow modelling fondant
- Icing sugar, for dusting

EXTRA EQUIPMENT

You will need a 6cm (2½in.) and a 4cm (1½in.) hibiscus flower cutter, a rolling pin and a baking paintbrush.

METHOD

For the orange biscuits:

Preheat the oven to 180°C and line two baking trays with baking paper.

Put the butter and sugar in a bowl and cream together until smooth, then add the egg, vanilla extract and orange zest and mix well. Gradually add the flour, salt and baking powder and mix to combine into a dough.

On a floured work surface, roll the dough out to a thickness of about 5mm, then cut out your hibiscus flower shapes using the 6cm (2½in.) cutter. You will need to re-roll the leftover dough a few times to cut out all 12 biscuits.

Place the flowers on the lined baking trays, ensuring they are a little spaced out to allow for spreading, then bake for about 10–12 minutes until light golden brown.

Leave to cool on a wire rack.

If you want to make these ahead of decorating, they will keep for 2–3 days in an airtight container stored at room temperature.

For the icing decorations:

Starting with your orange, purple or hot-pink modelling fondant, dust a surface with a little icing sugar then roll out the fondant till it's the thickness of card.

Cut out four shapes using your 6cm (2½in.) hibiscus flower cutter then leave to one side and repeat with the other two colours.

Next, roll out the white fondant and cut out 12 shapes using the smaller 4cm (1½in.) hibiscus flower cutter.

For each coloured flower, stick a white flower on top of it by using a bit of water and a small, clean baking paintbrush.

To make the stamen, take a small piece of yellow fondant and roll it into a little sausage shape, stick it down with a little water so it curves out, then add a few tiny balls of yellow fondant around it.

Repeat this until you have decorated all 12 biscuits.

You can leave these in an airtight container for 2–3 days but they are best eaten within 24 hours.

🍍 BANANA MACARONS 🍍

There's no time to monkey around when making these moreish treats. You might want to think about making two batches as they'll be gone in a peel of a banana!

Makes: 12 🍍 Time: 2 hours 🍍 Difficulty rating: 🦩🦩🦩

INGREDIENTS

For the macaron shells:

* 70g ground almonds
* 140g icing sugar
* 2 egg whites, at room temperature
* Yellow gel food colouring
* 50g caster sugar
* 100g dark chocolate

For the chocolate and hazelnut buttercream:

* 100g butter, softened
* 1 tsp vanilla extract
* 150g icing sugar
* 50g cocoa powder
* 4 tbsp hazelnut spread

EXTRA EQUIPMENT

You will need a standing mixer or handheld electric whisk, two baking trays, two piping bags, a small round-tip piping nozzle and a small open-star piping nozzle. To decorate, you will need a piping bag and writing-tip nozzle.

METHOD

For the macaron shells:

Preheat the oven to 140–150°C, line two baking trays with baking paper and set aside.

Place the ground almonds and icing sugar in a standing mixer or use a handheld electric whisk and blitz for about a minute, then transfer to a mixing bowl.

Beat one of the egg whites into the almond and icing sugar mixture to make a smooth paste. Add a few drops of yellow gel food colouring and mix to combine fully, then cover the bowl with a tea towel.

Pour the second egg white into a super-clean bowl and begin to whisk on high speed to form peaks. Gradually add the caster sugar 1 tablespoon at a time, until it starts to stiffen. Once all the sugar has been added, continue beating on a high setting for 2 minutes until the mixture resembles stiff, glossy peaks.

Add the egg-white mixture to the almond paste and, using a spatula, fold the two together from the bottom up. Continue that motion around 15–20 times until the mixture is fully incorporated and flows like molten lava.

Transfer the mixture into a piping bag fitted with a small round-tip nozzle and pipe 24 banana shapes on to the two lined baking trays. The mixture will spread so pipe to around 50 per cent of the size you want.

Tap the trays on a work surface a few times to release any air bubbles, then leave them to dry for 30 minutes. They will be ready to bake when they are no longer sticky or wet when touched.

Bake on the middle shelf of the oven for 8 minutes. Open the oven to let out any steam and turn the trays around, then bake for a further 8 minutes until the tops are crisp.

Leave them to cool fully before removing from the baking sheet.

To decorate the macarons, melt the chocolate by breaking it into small pieces and placing it in a heatproof bowl over a pan of simmering water. Stir occasionally until the chocolate has melted down completely then take off the heat to cool down to room temperature.

Fit a piping bag with a writing-tip nozzle and fill it with melted dark chocolate. Pipe lines of chocolate on to half of the banana shells and leave them to dry.

For the chocolate and hazelnut buttercream:

Cream together the butter, vanilla extract, icing sugar, cocoa powder and hazelnut spread until smooth and fluffy.

Transfer to a piping bag fitted with a small open-star nozzle and pipe the buttercream on to the undecorated macaron shells, placing the decorated macaron shells on top.

Leave in the fridge for 30 minutes before serving.

These will store in an airtight container for a few days if kept in the fridge.

🍍 WATERMELON BISCUITS 🍍

Biscuits disguised as fruit are the best kind of biscuits.
*Note: they do **not** count as one of your five a day.*

Makes: 12 🍍 Time: 2 hours, plus 2 hours' chilling time 🍍
Difficulty rating: 🦩🦩

INGREDIENTS

* 100g butter, softened
* 100g caster sugar
* 1 large egg
* ½ tsp vanilla extract
* 250g plain flour, plus extra for flouring
* ½ tsp baking powder
* ¼ tsp salt
* Red gel food colouring
* Green gel food colouring
* Cacao nibs

METHOD

Cream the butter and sugar in a large bowl until light and fluffy, then add the egg and vanilla extract and combine.

In another bowl, mix together the flour, baking powder and salt, then gradually add this to the butter and sugar mixture until you have dough.

Reserve approximately 100g dough and leave to one side, then add a few drops of red gel food colouring to the remaining dough and knead until fully coloured.

Shape the red dough into a 15cm x 7cm (6in. x 2¾in.) rectangle then roll it widthways and wrap in cling film.

Take 40g of the reserved dough and add a few drops of green gel food colouring, kneading it until fully coloured. Wrap the green dough and remaining plain dough separately in cling film and put all dough into the fridge for 2 hours.

On a lightly floured surface, roll the plain dough into a 15cm x 7cm (6in. x 2¾in.) rectangle. Remove the cling film from the red dough and then place it widthways on to the plain dough.

Wrap the plain dough over the red dough until it's fully covered and smooth it out so no red dough is showing.

Repeat this step with the green dough but roll it out into a 20cm x 7cm (8in. x 2¾in.) rectangle before wrapping it around the plain and red dough.

Cover the dough in cling film and leave in the fridge for another 2 hours until firm.

Preheat oven to 160°C, then unwrap the dough and slice it into six 1cm-thick circles with a sharp knife. Place them on to baking trays lined with baking paper, making sure they have enough space to expand a little when in the oven.

Lightly press six cacao nibs into each round of dough, allowing a little gap along the diameter of the circles as they will be cut in half once baked.

Bake for 9–11 minutes, checking carefully that they don't over-brown, then remove from the oven and immediately cut them in half on the baking trays.

Transfer the segments on to a wire rack and leave to cool completely.

These will keep for 2–3 days at room temperature in an airtight container.

☙ COCONUT AND LIME COOKIES ☙

These cookies are bursting with flavour – from the tang of the lime to the silkiness of the coconut and white chocolate, they will go down a treat at any social event.

Makes: 12 ☙ Time: 45 minutes ☙ Difficulty rating: 🦩🦩

INGREDIENTS

* 125g butter
* 225g caster sugar
* 1 egg
* 1 tsp vanilla extract
* 150g plain flour
* 150g self-raising flour
* Zest of 2 limes
* 80g desiccated coconut
* 100g white chocolate, chopped into small pieces

METHOD

Preheat the oven to 180°C and line two baking trays with baking paper.

Cream the butter and sugar in a large bowl until light and fluffy, then add the egg and vanilla extract and combine.

In another bowl, combine the two flours, then add half to the butter and sugar mixture and mix it through. Add the remaining flour and combine it all together, then add the lime zest, desiccated coconut and the white chocolate and fold it all together.

Place spoonfuls of the dough on the lined baking trays, leaving enough space around each for them to expand when cooking.

Flatten each ball out a little with the palm of your hand then bake in the oven for 10 minutes.

Remove from the oven and transfer the cookies to a wire rack to cool.

These will keep in an airtight container for 2–3 days.

🍍 FLAMINGO FIZZ MACARONS 🍍

Let's get fizzy with Flamia the Flamingo's macarons,
featuring her favourite secret ingredient.

Makes: 12 🍍 Time: 2 hours 🍍 Difficulty rating: 🦩🦩🦩

INGREDIENTS

**For the strawberry
macaron shells:**

- 70g ground almonds
- 140g icing sugar
- 50g freeze-dried
  strawberries
- 2 egg whites, at room
  temperature
- Pink gel food colouring
- 50g caster sugar

For the marble icing topping:

- 100g royal icing sugar
- 3 tbsp water
- Pink gel food colouring

**For the strawberry
buttercream:**

- 100g butter, softened
- 200g icing sugar
- 50g freeze-dried
  strawberries
- 2 tbsp popping candy

EXTRA EQUIPMENT

You will need a standing mixer or handheld electric whisk, two
piping bags, a small round-tip piping nozzle and a small open-star
piping nozzle.

METHOD

For the strawberry macaron shells:

Preheat the oven to 140–150°C, line two baking trays with baking
paper and set aside.

Place the ground almonds, icing sugar and freeze-dried
strawberries in a standing mixer or use a handheld electric whisk
and blitz for about a minute, then transfer to a mixing bowl.

Beat one of the egg whites into the almond and icing sugar
mixture to make a smooth paste. Add a few drops of pink gel
food colouring and mix to combine fully, then cover the bowl with
a tea towel.

Pour the second egg white into a super-clean bowl and begin
to whisk on high speed to form peaks. Gradually add the caster
sugar 1 tablespoon at a time, until it starts to stiffen. Once all the
sugar has been added, continue beating on a high setting for 2
minutes until the mixture resembles stiff, glossy peaks.

Add the egg-white mixture to the almond paste and, using a
spatula, fold the two together from the bottom up. Continue that
motion around 15–20 times until the mixture is fully incorporated
and flows like molten lava.

Transfer the mixture into a piping bag fitted with a small round-tip nozzle and pipe 24 rounds on to the two lined baking trays. The mixture will spread so pipe to around 50 per cent of the size you want.

Tap the trays on a work surface a few times to release any air bubbles, then leave them to dry for 30 minutes. They will be ready to bake when they are no longer sticky or wet when touched.

Bake on the middle shelf of the oven for 8 minutes. Open the oven to let out any steam and turn the trays around, then bake for a further 8 minutes until the tops are crisp.

Leave them to cool fully before removing from the baking sheet.

For the marble icing topping:

Once the macaron shells are fully cooled, make the icing by adding the royal icing sugar and water to a bowl and mixing until you have a consistency that is thick enough to coat the back of a spoon and thin enough to fall off a spoon easily.

Add a few drops of pink gel food colouring and swirl it around the icing, not mixing it in but just to create a marble pattern.

To decorate, dip half the shells rounded side down into the icing then twist and lift them out, revealing the marble pattern.

Leave them aside for an hour for the icing to set.

For the strawberry buttercream:

Cream together the butter, icing sugar and freeze-dried strawberries until smooth and fluffy.

Transfer to a piping bag fitted with a small open-star nozzle and pipe the buttercream on to the flat ends of the plain macaron shells.

Sprinkle some popping candy on top then sandwich them together with the decorated shells. Leave in the fridge for 30 minutes before serving.

These will store in an airtight container for a few days if kept in the fridge.

BARS
AND
BITES

TROPICAL CARROT CAKE SQUARES

*Give your carrot cake a tropical twist and make your afternoon teas
a summery affair (even in the middle of winter!).*

Makes: 12 squares ⚘ **Time: 2 hours** ⚘ **Difficulty rating:** 🦩🦩

INGREDIENTS

For the carrot cake:

- 75g pistachio nuts
- 150ml sunflower oil
- 175g light muscovado sugar
- 2 eggs
- 225g self-raising flour
- 1 tsp baking powder
- 1 tbsp ground cinnamon
- 1 tsp ground ginger
- ¼ tsp fine sea salt
- 300g carrots, peeled and coarsely grated
- 50g desiccated coconut
- 50g dried mango, chopped
- 100g tropical dried fruit mix

For the icing:

- 150g full-fat cream cheese
- 3 tbsp icing sugar
- 125ml coconut cream, chilled

For the topping:

- 20g coconut flakes
- 25g dried mango, chopped
- 25g pistachio nuts, blitzed
- 25g dried papaya, chopped
- Zest of 1 lime

EXTRA EQUIPMENT

You will need a 20cm (8in.) square cake tin and a standing mixer.

METHOD

For the carrot cake:

Preheat the oven to 170°C and line a 20cm (8in.) square cake tin with baking paper.

Pour 75g pistachios into a standing mixer and blitz until coarsely chopped.

Whisk together the oil, sugar and eggs in a large mixing bowl for 2 minutes until frothy, then sift in the flour, baking powder, spices and salt and combine until smooth.

Add the grated carrots, coconut, mango and dried fruit and mix to combine well.

Pour the cake batter into the prepared tin and smooth into the corners. Bake for 50–60 minutes, or until set and springy in the centre, then remove from the oven.

Cool in the tin for 15 minutes, then turn out and leave to cool completely on a wire rack before icing.

For the icing:
Whisk together the cream cheese and icing sugar until smooth, then add the chilled coconut cream and whisk until thick and spreadable.

To decorate, spread the icing thickly on top of the cake, making rough peaks, then scatter over the topping ingredients and cut into squares.

These will keep for up to a week if kept in an airtight container.

PINEAPPLE UPSIDE-DOWN TRAY BAKE

When life gives you pineapples (or you have to go to a shop to buy them), make an upside-down cake!

Makes: 6   Time: 2 hours   Difficulty rating:

INGREDIENTS

* 250g golden syrup
* 6 tinned pineapple rings
* 6 glacé cherries
* 300g butter
* 300g caster sugar
* 4 eggs
* 300g self-raising flour

EXTRA EQUIPMENT

You will need a deep 30cm x 20cm (12in. x 8in.) rimmed baking tin.

METHOD

Preheat the oven to 180°C then line the 30cm x 20cm (12in. x 8in.) baking tin.

Melt the golden syrup in a pan then pour it into the tin, spreading it out until even.

Lay out the six pineapple rings into two rows of three and put a glacé cherry in the middle of each ring. Put the tin to one side.

Place the butter and sugar in a large bowl and beat the two together until pale and fluffy. Gradually add the eggs one by one, mixing in between each addition, then fold in the flour until the batter is smooth.

Pour the mixture into the prepared tin and spread it out so that the surface is level.

Bake for 35–40 minutes until golden, then leave to cool in the tin for 30 minutes.

To serve, carefully turn the baking tray upside down on a chopping board or serving dish to reveal the cake, then cut into six squares and serve warm.

☙ FLAMILLIONAIRE SHORTBREAD ☙

Flamia the Flamingo is just too good to us. This time she's sharing her recipe for shortbread treats that are the perfect accompaniment to afternoon tea.

Makes: 12 ☙ Time: 2–3 hours ☙ Difficulty rating: 🦩

INGREDIENTS

For the shortbread base:

- 250g plain flour
- 75g caster sugar
- 175g butter, softened

For the caramel:

- 100g butter
- 100g light brown sugar
- 2 x 397g cans condensed milk

For the chocolate topping:

- 100g milk chocolate
- 100g dark chocolate
- 50g white chocolate
- A few drops pink gel food colouring

EXTRA EQUIPMENT

You will need a 30cm x 20cm (12in. x 8in.) baking tin.

METHOD

For the shortbread base:

Preheat the oven to 180°C and line a 30cm x 20cm (12in. x 8in.) baking tin.

Mix the flour and caster sugar in a large bowl, then add the butter and rub the mixture together with your fingers until it resembles breadcrumbs.

Bring the mixture together so it forms a dough then press it evenly into the base of the prepared tin.

Prick the dough a few times with a fork then bake for 20 minutes, until lightly browned, then leave to cool in the tin while you make the caramel.

For the caramel:

Put the butter, light brown sugar and two 397g cans of condensed milk into a medium pan and gently heat until the sugar has dissolved.

Bring the mixture to the boil, then reduce the heat and simmer, stirring at all times, for about 5–10 minutes until the mixture has thickened.

Immediately pour over the shortbread base and leave to cool for an hour.

For the chocolate topping:

Put the milk and dark chocolate into a heatproof bowl and set it over a pan of simmering water. Let them melt, stirring the two chocolates together, then pour them over the cooled caramel.

Repeat the above in a clean bowl and melt the white chocolate but, once melted, add a few drops of pink food colouring and mix it through.

Drizzle the now pink chocolate over the top of the milk/dark chocolate then, using a toothpick or the tip of a knife, swirl the two chocolates together until you have a marble effect.

Leave aside to cool, then cut into 12 squares and serve.

MANGO MACAROONS

Taste the tropics with these mango, coconut and white chocolate bite-sized biscuits.

Makes: 12 🍍 **Time: 45 minutes** 🍍 **Difficulty rating:** 🦩

INGREDIENTS

- 2 egg whites
- 60g caster sugar
- 1 tsp vanilla extract
- Pinch of salt
- 200g desiccated coconut
- 50g dried mango, cut into small pieces
- 100g white chocolate

EXTRA EQUIPMENT

You will need an electric whisk and an ice-cream scoop.

METHOD

Preheat the oven to 160°C and line a baking tray with baking paper.

Add the egg whites and sugar to a large mixing bowl and whisk together on a medium speed, until thick. Stir in the vanilla extract and salt, then add the desiccated coconut and dried mango and combine it all together.

Using a small ice-cream scoop or teaspoon, spoon 12 balls of the mixture on to the prepared baking tray.

Bake in the oven for 10–15 minutes, checking after 10 to ensure they're lightly toasted but not completely browned.

Remove from the oven and leave to cool on the tray.

Once fully cooled, dip the base of the macaroons into a bowl of melted white chocolate and return them to the baking tray for the chocolate to set.

These will keep for up to 1 week stored at room temperature in an airtight container or you can freeze them in a sealed container for up to 3 months.

🍍 TROPICAL ROCKY ROAD 🍍

*Just like the life hidden deep in rainforests,
this rocky road has lots of hidden gems in it.*

Makes: 12 🍍 **Time: 2 hours** 🍍 **Difficulty rating:** 🦩

INGREDIENTS

* 400g white chocolate
* 100g coconut oil, melted
* 150g white mini marshmallows
* 100g desiccated coconut
* 80g dried papaya cubes
* 80g dried pineapple cubes
* 80g red glacé cherries
* 100g pistachio nuts, de-shelled

EXTRA EQUIPMENT

You will need a 20cm x 30cm (12in. x 8in.) baking tray.

METHOD

Line a 20cm x 30cm (12in. x 8in.) baking tray and set aside.

Put the white chocolate in a large bowl set over a pan of simmering water and heat gently until the chocolate is fully melted.

Add the melted coconut oil and stir together, then remove the bowl from the heat and set aside.

In another large bowl, combine all but a handful of the dry ingredients, then pour the melted chocolate over the top and stir it all together.

Spread the mixture out in the prepared tray then sprinkle over the remaining handful of dry ingredients to decorate.

Place in the fridge to set for 30 minutes, then remove and cut into 12 bars.

🍍 FLAMINGO CHOUXNUTS 🍍

Chouxnut? Choux-what?! A chouxnut is choux pastry, shaped like a doughnut and filled with crème patissière. They're almost as in vogue as flamingos, and together they're as fabulous and feathery as only a flamingo chouxnut can be!

Serves: 8 🍍 **Time: 1 hour 45 minutes** 🍍 **Difficulty rating:** 🦩🦩

INGREDIENTS

For the chouxnuts:

* 120g butter
* 250ml water
* 150g plain flour
* 1 tsp vanilla extract
* 4 eggs

For the raspberry crème patissière:

* 400ml full-fat milk
* 2 tbsp freeze-dried raspberry powder
* 100g caster sugar
* 4 egg yolks
* 40g cornflour
* 40g butter, cubed

For the decoration:

* 100g flaked coconut
* 4 drops pink gel food colouring
* 200g white chocolate

EXTRA EQUIPMENT

You will need a 20cm (8in.) saucepan, a sandwich bag, two piping bags, a round-tip piping nozzle and a filler nozzle.

METHOD

For the chouxnuts:

Preheat the oven to 200°C and line two baking trays with baking paper.

Heat the butter and water together in a 20cm (8in.) saucepan until the mixture begins to boil.

Remove from the heat, then beat in the flour all at once with a wooden spoon until the mixture comes together and peels away from the pan.

Add the vanilla extract and then the eggs one at a time and beat well after each addition, until the dough is elastic and shiny.

Fit a piping bag with a round-tip nozzle and fill it with the dough, then pipe 5–7cm (2–3in.) diameter rings on to the prepared baking trays.

Bake for 20-25 minutes until golden and they sound hollow when tapped, then switch off the oven, propping open the door with a wooden spoon to let the pastry dry out for a few more minutes.

Remove from the oven, then allow to cool completely on a wire rack.

Once cool, the pastries can be kept at room temperature for up to one week in an airtight container or you can freeze them for up to 1 month.

For the raspberry crème patissière:

Pour the milk and raspberry powder into a pan and bring the mixture to the boil. Once it begins boiling, remove it from the heat.

Whisk the sugar, egg yolks and cornflour together in a large bowl, then pour a little of the hot milk over the egg mixture and whisk continuously.

Continue with the rest of the hot milk until well combined, then return to the pan.

Over a gentle heat, stir the mixture continuously for a few minutes until it thickens and just starts to boil, then remove from the heat and pass it through a sieve into a clean bowl.

Add the butter to the mixture and stir until melted, then leave to cool.

When ready, spoon the mixture into a piping bag fitted with a filler nozzle.

Make a small hole in each of the chouxnuts then insert the filler nozzle and fill them with the desired amount of crème patissière, being careful not to overfill or they'll burst.

For the decoration:

Pour the coconut flakes into a sandwich bag and add two drops of pink gel food colouring.

Seal the bag and shake it around as much as you can until the coconut flakes are tinted pink, then pour them into a bowl and leave to one side.

Melt the white chocolate by breaking it into small pieces and placing it in a heatproof bowl over a pan of simmering water. Stir occasionally, until the chocolate has melted down completely, and take off the heat.

Add two drops of pink gel food colouring to the chocolate and mix it through until it has been tinted a pastel pink colour.

Dip one flat side of each of the chouxnuts into the pink white chocolate, then sprinkle over some pink coconut flakes and leave for the chocolate to set.

These are best eaten fresh on the day so serve immediately.

PARTY
FOOD

"TROPIC LIKE IT'S HOT" LOLLIES

The tropical heat is tiring. Make sure you have a stash of these ice lollies
in your freezer for when you are in need of an energy boost.

Makes: 8 🍍 **Time: 15 minutes plus 4 hours' freezing time** 🍍 **Difficulty rating:**

INGREDIENTS

* 2 kiwi fruit
* 2 passion fruit
* 500ml pineapple juice

EXTRA EQUIPMENT

You will need eight ice-lolly moulds and a jug.

METHOD

Peel the kiwi fruit to remove all the fuzzy skin, then thinly slice them horizontally until you have eight segments that are all the same size per kiwi fruit.

Halve the passion fruit and remove all the seeds and juice into a bowl.

In a jug, pour 500ml pineapple juice, then add the passion fruit seeds and juice and mix it all around.

Take your ice-lolly moulds and stick one slice of kiwi fruit to each side.

Carefully pour the mixture equally between the moulds.

If your lolly moulds have lids with the lolly sticks attached, you will need to place the lids on top before leaving to set flat in the fridge.

If you wish to use wooden lolly sticks instead, cover the mould in tinfoil and carefully pierce a hole in the foil through to the lolly mixture. The foil will ensure the stick remains in the central position as the mixture sets.

Leave to set in the freezer on a flat surface for up to 4 hours or overnight.

To remove the lollies, dip the moulds in warm water for a few seconds then gently wriggle and ease the ice lollies out.

🍍 WATERMELON MERINGUE POPS 🍍

*If you are in need of a sugar boost to get you through the day,
these are definitely your go-to super-sweet treat.*

Makes: 8 🍍 Time: 1 hour 30 minutes 🍍 Difficulty rating: 🦩

INGREDIENTS

* 4 egg whites
* 200g caster sugar
* Pinch of salt
* 1 tsp vanilla extract
* Pink and green gel food colouring
* A handful of poppy seeds

EXTRA EQUIPMENT

You will need an electric mixer, eight wooden lolly sticks, two large piping bags, a closed-star nozzle and an open-star nozzle.

METHOD

Preheat the oven to 150°C and line two large baking trays with baking paper. Lay out your lolly sticks on the paper, about 7cm (2¾in.) apart, and set the trays aside.

Add egg whites to a large mixing bowl, then add the sugar, salt and vanilla extract.

Whisk the mixture together on a medium speed until it forms white, thick, stiff meringue peaks.

Divide the mixture 70/30 between two bowls and gently colour the larger quantity pink and the smaller quantity green, being careful when folding the colour through so you don't over-deflate the meringue mixture.

Take two large piping bags and fit one with a closed-star nozzle and one with an open-star nozzle.

Add the pink mixture to the piping bag with the open-star nozzle and the green mixture to the piping bag fitted with the closed-star nozzle.

Using the pink meringue mixture, pipe in an "S" formation directly on to the baking paper, starting 5cm (2in.) past one end of the lolly stick and increasing the width of the "S" shapes as you go, until you're approximately halfway down the lolly stick.

Continue with all the lolly sticks that have been laid out then pipe a curved line with the green meringue beneath the pink meringue, ensuring you have left enough lolly stick at the bottom for it to be held.

Scatter the pink meringue with some poppy seeds then bake for 1 hour, rotating the trays after 30 minutes, until the meringue is dry, crisp and easily pulls away from the baking paper.

Once baked, turn off the oven and prop the door open, leaving the meringues inside to cool. *Note: this is what makes them nice and chewy.*

These are best served the same day as baking, but will last 2 weeks if kept in an airtight container.

 PARADISE PIZZA

*Pizzas are great. But sweet pizzas topped with yoghurt
and a medley of fruit are the best!*

Makes: 8   Time: 30 minutes   Difficulty rating:

INGREDIENTS

* 1 ready-made
  pizza base
* 1 kiwi fruit
* 5 strawberries, sliced
* ½ a fresh mango
* 2 tbsp Greek yoghurt
* 1 tbsp desiccated
  coconut

METHOD

Place the ready-made pizza base on to a baking tray and bake in the oven, following the packaging's cooking instructions.

Remove and leave to cool for 10 minutes while you prepare the fruit.

Peel and slice a kiwi fruit, hull and slice a few strawberries and halve a mango, cutting the fruit into small chunks.

Take the slightly cooled pizza base and spread the Greek yoghurt across it. Top with the pieces of fruit then sprinkle over some desiccated coconut before cutting into eight slices.

🍍 TROPICANA SPRINKLES 🍍

*Get tropi-tastic and bring an abundance of joy to your baking
every day with these crazily colourful sprinkles.*

Makes: 200g sprinkles 🍍 Time: 5 minutes 🍍 Difficulty rating: 🦩

INGREDIENTS

* 50g bright rainbow hundreds and thousands
* 50g edible star-shaped confetti sprinkles
* 40g rainbow sugar-coated chocolate sprinkles
* 30g rainbow dragées (sugar balls)
* 30g yellow sugar crystals

EXTRA EQUIPMENT

You will need an airtight container.

METHOD

Add each type of sprinkle into a large bowl and combine them well.

Using a teaspoon, spoon the mixture into an airtight container and give it a little shake.

Use these colourful sprinkles to add some tropical flare to any sweet treats, adding instant jazz.

These will keep in an airtight container for at least 3 years.

 BANANA SUSHI

If you aren't a lover of traditional sushi, try this banana-licious version covered in all sorts of sweet treats.

Serves: 5–10 　 Time: 45 minutes 　 Difficulty rating:

INGREDIENTS

* Desiccated coconut
* Toasted almonds
* Freeze-dried strawberries
* Tropicana Sprinkles (see page 87)
* 4 bananas
* Hazelnut spread
* Biscuit spread

EXTRA EQUIPMENT

You will need five rimmed baking trays.

METHOD

Line a baking tray with a piece of baking paper then place the coconut, toasted almonds, freeze-dried strawberries and sprinkles separately in the other four baking trays ready for decorating.

Peel one banana and, using a knife, cover it in hazelnut spread. *Warning: this is messy work so have a cloth ready to wipe your hands.*

As soon as the banana is coated, roll it in the desiccated coconut and place on the lined baking tray.

Repeat the above but roll the second banana in the freeze-dried strawberries and the third in the sprinkles.

For the final banana, coat it in the biscuit spread and cover it with the toasted almonds.

Put the bananas in the fridge to set for 30 minutes then remove and slice into sushi-sized bites.

Serve on a tray with chopsticks for an authentic tropical sushi feel.

🍍 BUTTERFLY BISCUITS 🍍

Either decorate them yourself or bake the biscuits and get your friends and family over to ice their very own edible butterflies. It's the perfect excuse to get everyone together.

Makes: 16 🍍 Time: 2 hours 🍍 Difficulty rating: 🦩🦩

INGREDIENTS

For the orange biscuits:

* 85g unsalted butter
* 100g golden caster sugar
* 1 egg
* ½ tsp vanilla extract
* Zest of 1 orange
* 200g plain flour, plus extra for dusting
* ¼ tsp salt
* ½ tsp baking powder

For the icing:

* 900g royal icing
* 150ml cold water
* Gel food colouring (pink, blue and black)

EXTRA EQUIPMENT

You will need a butterfly cutter, a rolling pin, piping bags, a writing-tip piping nozzle, a squeezy piping bottle (optional) and cocktail sticks.

METHOD

For the orange biscuits:

Preheat the oven to 180°C and line two baking trays with baking paper.

Put the butter and sugar in a bowl and cream together until smooth, then add the egg, vanilla extract and orange zest and mix well. Gradually add the flour, salt and baking powder and mix to combine into a dough.

On a floured work surface, roll the dough out to a thickness of about 5mm, then cut out your butterfly shapes. You will need to re-roll the leftover dough a few times to cut out all 16 biscuits.

Place the butterflies on the lined baking trays, ensuring they are a little spaced out to allow for spreading, then bake for about 10–12 minutes until light golden brown.

Leave to cool on a wire rack.

If you want to make these ahead of decorating, they will keep for 2–3 days in an airtight container stored at room temperature.

For the icing:

Pour the cold water into a large bowl and add all the icing sugar.

Combine the two together, slowly at first to avoid a sugar cloud, then beat for around 5 minutes until the mixture is bright white and the consistency of toothpaste.

Divide into bowls for your desired colours and colour each to your desired tone.

Line icing:

Line icing should be the texture of toothpaste.

To line your biscuits, fit a piping bag with a writing-tip piping nozzle and fill it with your desired icing tone. Pipe around your butterfly shapes, making sure that you join up your trail to form an unbroken wall. Let the walls dry for about 5 minutes before filling with flood icing.

Flood icing:

To create flood icing, add a little bit more water to create a slightly looser consistency to the line icing mix.

Tip: don't add too much water in one go. Take it a few drops at a time to ensure you don't add too much and consequently ruin the icing.

You can pipe the flood icing using a squeezy piping bottle or a piping bag – simply fill them with the icing and carefully fill the area you wish to colour. Don't add too much as you can spread it out with a cocktail stick – if you fill too much it could overflow the lines.

To create the butterfly wing pattern, pipe around the butterfly shape using some black flood icing, then fill in the rest using blue or pink flood icing.

To create the marble effect, once you have flooded your biscuits, use a cocktail stick to bring the black icing into the blue or pink colour. Try to make it as even as you can on both sides.

Leave the icing to dry for 30 minutes before serving.

BREAKFAST

 ALOHA SMOOTHIE

Cool down on a hot day with this healthy, delicious smoothie.

Serves: 2   Time: 15 minutes   Difficulty rating:

INGREDIENTS

* 1 banana
* 50g strawberries
* 100g frozen mango
* 100ml coconut yoghurt
* 50ml coconut milk

EXTRA EQUIPMENT

You will need a blender.

METHOD

Put all the ingredients into a blender and blitz until smooth, adding a splash more coconut milk if required.

Divide the smoothie between two glasses and garnish each glass with a strawberry.

☙ PASSION FRUIT PANCAKES ☙

These are the yummiest breakfast treat for lazy Sundays.
In fact, they are so yummy that you'll want them
for breakfast, lunch and dinner.

Serves: 4 ☙ Time: 30 minutes ☙ Difficulty rating: 🦩

INGREDIENTS

For the pancakes:

* 3 passion fruit
* 250g self-raising flour
* 50g desiccated coconut
* 1 tsp salt
* 1 tsp baking powder
* 100g brown sugar
* 250ml milk
* 2 eggs
* 20g butter or coconut oil, for frying

For the topping:

* Coconut yoghurt
* Juice of 1 passion fruit
* Desiccated coconut
* Banana chips

EXTRA EQUIPMENT

You will need a large non-stick frying pan.

METHOD

Preheat your oven to 100ºC.

Cut open the passion fruit, and scoop all the juice and seeds out into a sieve set over a bowl. Press the seeds and juice down with the back of a spoon until you have 4 tablespoons' worth of juice. Set the juice aside.

Sift together the flour, desiccated coconut, salt, baking powder and sugar in a large bowl. Make a well in the centre, pour in the milk, then add the eggs and passion fruit juice and whisk until the pancake batter is smooth. Pour the batter into a clean measuring jug.

Heat a frying pan over a medium heat and lightly grease it with butter or coconut oil.

When the butter or oil has melted, pour 2–3 rounds, each approximately 10cm (4in.) in diameter, of the pancake batter into the pan; the mixture will spread out so take care to keep it as circular as you can.

Cook each pancake on one side until bubbles appear on the surface, then flip with a spatula and cook for 30 seconds more on the reverse side. Set aside the cooked pancakes on a heatproof plate and put into your oven to keep them warm.

Continue with the remaining batter until all the pancakes have been cooked.

To serve, stack four pancakes on top of each other, finished with a dollop of coconut yoghurt, a drizzle of passion fruit juice, some desiccated coconut and a few banana chips.

🍍 TROPICAL GRANOLA 🍍

*It's time for some nutty goodness with this granola
that'll make your mornings less dreary and more dazzle.*

Serves: 8 🍍 Time: 1 hour 🍍 Difficulty rating: 🦩

INGREDIENTS

* 400g rolled oats
* 100g pecans
* 100g toasted almonds
* 1 tsp fine sea salt
* ½ tsp ground cinnamon
* 100ml coconut oil
* 100ml maple syrup
* 1 tsp vanilla extract
* 100g tropical fruit mix (dried papaya, pineapple, mango and currants)
* 50g banana chips

EXTRA EQUIPMENT

You will need a large bowl and a large, rimmed baking tray.

METHOD

Preheat your oven to 180ºC and line a large, rimmed baking tray with baking paper.

In a large mixing bowl, combine the oats, nuts, salt and cinnamon then stir well.

Pour in the oil, maple syrup and vanilla extract and mix well until every oat and nut is lightly coated.

Pour the granola on to the prepared baking tray and use a large spoon to spread it into an even layer.

Bake for 24 minutes until lightly golden, stirring halfway to ensure all the oats crisp up, although it will further crisp up as it cools.

Let the granola cool completely for 30 minutes, then top with the dried tropical fruits and banana chips. Break the granola into pieces with your hands if you want big chunks, or stir it around with a spoon if you prefer finer granola.

This will keep for up to 4 weeks if stored in an airtight container at room temperature. If you want to batch bake and freeze, store it in a sealed freezer bag in the freezer for up to 3 months. The dried fruit can freeze solid, so let it warm to room temperature for 5–10 minutes before serving.

To serve, add your choice of yoghurt or milk then top with fresh berries and a drizzle of honey.

FLAMIN-GO ENERGY BITES

*Get up and flamin-GO with these tasty, healthy energy balls,
perfect for breakfast or as a snack.*

Makes: 20 ♨ Time: 30 minutes ♨ Difficulty rating: 🦩

INGREDIENTS

* 100g flaked almonds
* 100g coconut flakes
* 8 pitted medjool dates
* 1 tsp honey
* 1 tsp vanilla extract
* 100g freeze-dried strawberries

EXTRA EQUIPMENT

You will need a standing mixer.

METHOD

Add the almonds and coconut flakes to a standing mixer and blitz until they are coarsely ground.

Add in the remaining ingredients and blitz until everything starts to come together in a ball, scraping down the sides of the bowl as needed.

Scoop a small tablespoon of mixture into the palm of your hand and roll it into a ball. Repeat until you have used up all of the mixture.

Store them in an airtight container in the fridge for up to 1 week or freeze them for up to 3 months.

🍍 PARADISE ON TOAST 🍍

Swap your boring buttered toast for this perfect pick-me-up.

Serves: 1 🍍 Time: 15 minutes 🍍 Difficulty rating: 🦩

INGREDIENTS

* 2 tbsp coconut flakes
* 2 slices of sourdough
* 2 tbsp peanut butter
* 1 banana, sliced
* Honey

METHOD

Preheat the oven to 150°C and lay out the flaked coconut on a flat baking tray.

Toast in the oven for 5–10 minutes, checking throughout, until the coconut is lightly browned. *Note: be sure to check often as the flakes can turn brown quickly depending on your oven.*

Once toasted, remove from the oven and leave to cool.

Meanwhile, pop the slices of sourdough under a grill or in a toaster until golden.

Leave to cool a little, then spread over a generous amount of peanut butter.

Evenly spread the banana slices across the sourdough, then sprinkle the toasted coconut on top.

Finish with a drizzle of honey and serve.

DESSERTS

🍍 WATERMELON SWISS ROLL 🍍

Serves: 6–8 🍍 Time: 1 hour 🍍 Difficulty rating: 🦩🦩

INGREDIENTS

For the vanilla sponge:

* Vegetable oil, for greasing
* 3 eggs
* 125g caster sugar, plus extra for dusting
* 125g plain flour
* ½ tsp vanilla extract
* Pink gel food colouring
* Green gel food colouring

For the filling:

* 120ml double cream
* Chocolate chips

For the decoration:

* Chocolate chips

EXTRA EQUIPMENT

You will need a Swiss roll baking tin or shallow baking tin and an electric whisk.

METHOD

For the vanilla sponge:

Preheat the oven to 170°C and line a Swiss roll tin or a shallow baking tin with baking paper. Lightly grease the baking paper with a little vegetable oil, then leave to one side.

In a large bowl, whisk together the eggs and caster sugar for around 5 minutes until the mixture is pale, thick and the consistency is like mousse.

Sift in the flour and add the vanilla extract into the mixture and gently fold them in – take your time with this as you don't want to lose any air.

Split the mixture evenly between two mixing bowls and gently fold pink gel food colouring into one bowl and green gel food colouring into the other bowl until they are fully tinted.

Pour the pink mixture on to one half of the prepared tin, using a spatula to smooth it out evenly, and pour and smooth out the green mixture on to the other half of the tin, leaving behind a few tablespoons.

Add a few more drops of your green gel food colouring to the remaining green mixture so it's darker, then drizzle lines of the darker green mixture across the light green batter in the tin. To create the watermelon skin pattern, use a knife or toothpick and pull it horizontally through both mixtures so you have zigzag lines.

 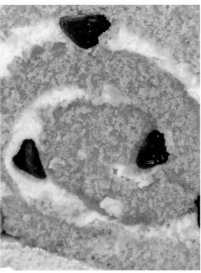 

Bake in the centre of the oven for 10–12 minutes, until risen and just firm to the touch.

Lay out a clean, damp cloth on the work surface followed by a piece of baking paper that is larger than the sponge. Dust the baking paper with caster sugar then run a knife around the edge of the warm sponge and turn it out on to the fresh sheet of baking paper, peeling the lining paper away from the cooked sponge.

While it is still warm, carefully roll the sponge (from the pink side so that it's pink on the inside and green on the outside) using the baking paper as support to lift it, then leave to cool in the rolled-up position.

For the filling and decoration:

Whisk the cream until thick and aerated.

When the sponge has fully cooled, unroll it and smooth out a thick layer of the whipped cream on to it, then sprinkle some chocolate chips over the top.

Gently re-roll the sponge starting from the pink side.

Cut the ends off to neaten the shape then add a few chocolate chips to look like watermelon seeds.

Eat within 24 hours.

FLAMIA'S RIPPLE ICE CREAM

Extra smooth, extra silky, extra sumptuous. Behold Flamia's ripple ice cream.

Serves: 8　　Time: 30 minutes plus 4 hours' freezing time
Difficulty rating:

INGREDIENTS

- 250g fresh raspberries
- 50g caster sugar
- 500ml double cream
- 397g tin condensed milk
- 2 tsp vanilla extract
- 8 waffle ice-cream cones
- Freeze-dried raspberries (optional)

EXTRA EQUIPMENT

You will need a 900g loaf tin.

METHOD

Put the raspberries and sugar into a medium pan and place over a medium heat. Simmer for about 5–10 minutes, stirring occasionally, until the raspberries have broken down.

Using a sieve, push the mixture into a large bowl until you have a vibrant sauce, then discard any remaining seeds and pulp. Allow to cool completely.

In a large mixing bowl, whip the double cream until stiff, then add the condensed milk and vanilla extract and fold them all together.

Pour half of the mixture into a 900g loaf tin then drizzle several tablespoons of the raspberry sauce on top. Swirl the sauce through with a toothpick or knife then pour on the rest of the ice-cream mixture and more raspberry sauce. If there is any sauce left you can use this later as an ice-cream topping.

Cover with cling film or foil then place in the freezer for at least 4 hours, or overnight, before serving.

To serve, leave it out for 10 minutes to melt a little before scooping out into waffle cones and sprinkling with freeze-dried raspberries.

✦ TOUCAN TACOS ✦

When toucans don't live on your doorstep, bring them (or at least an edible version!) closer to home with these delicious toucan tacos.

Makes: 6 ✦ Time: 45 minutes ✦ Difficulty rating: 🦩🦩

INGREDIENTS

For the tacos:

* 90g plain flour
* 20g cocoa powder
* 3 egg whites
* 130g icing sugar
* 60g unsalted butter
* ½ tsp vanilla extract

For the filling:

* 200ml double cream
* Mango, cubed
* Kiwi fruit, sliced
* 5 strawberries, chopped
* Zest of 1 lime

EXTRA EQUIPMENT

You will need a palette knife, a piping bag and an open-star nozzle.

METHOD

For the tacos:

Preheat the oven to 160°C and line a baking tray with baking paper. Draw six 20cm-wide (8in.-wide) circles on to the baking paper and leave to one side.

Sift the flour and cocoa powder together into a medium bowl.

In a separate bowl, whisk the egg whites and sugar together until smooth.

Add the dry mixture into the egg mixture, then melt the butter and add this and the vanilla extract, stirring it all together until combined.

Rest two wooden spoons across a large bowl and set aside for later.

Take the prepared baking tray and dollop a heaped tablespoon of taco batter in the centre of one of the drawn circles. Use a palette knife to smooth out the batter, removing any excess you don't need.

Continue to fill all the circles, then put the tray in the oven and bake for 8 minutes.

Remove the baking tray from the oven and place on a heatproof surface next to the wooden spoons. Working quickly, carefully lift

the tacos from the baking tray one by one using a spatula, draping them over the wooden spoons to create the taco shape. The tacos will harden almost immediately once out of the heat, which is why you need to work quickly! Leave the tacos draped over the spoons while you make the filling.

For the filling:

Add the double cream to a large bowl and whisk until it thickens.

Transfer the cream into a piping bag fitted with an open-star nozzle, then pipe a generous amount into each taco.

Top with fruit and a sprinkle of lime zest and serve immediately.

MANGO SORBET

Juicy, fruity and mouth-wateringly good, this sorbet will give you feel-good summer vibes all year round.

Serves: 8   Time: 10 minutes plus 2 hours' freezing time

Difficulty rating:

INGREDIENTS

* 240ml water
* 1 tbsp lime juice
* 150g granulated sugar
* 600g frozen mango chunks

EXTRA EQUIPMENT

You will need a jug, a food processor and a 900g loaf tin.

METHOD

In a medium pan, combine the water, lime juice and sugar and heat gently until the sugar has dissolved. Leave the mixture to cool.

Add the mango chunks and half of the cooled mixture to a food processor and blend until the mango is mashed.

Add the remaining mixture and blend again for 4 minutes until the mixture is smooth and creamy.

Pour the mixture into the loaf tin and freeze for 1–2 hours.

Before serving, let the sorbet soften for 5 minutes then serve into bowls.

This will keep in the freezer in an ice-cream container for 3 months.

🍍 COCONUT CHEESECAKE 🍍

*Impress your guests with this silky cheesecake – it's likely they'll
be round for more once they've tasted it.*

Makes: 6 🍍 Time: 1 hour, plus 1 hour for setting 🍍 Difficulty rating: 🦩

INGREDIENTS

- 2 x 400ml tins coconut milk
- 100g digestive biscuits
- 40g desiccated coconut
- 40g butter, melted
- 200g cream cheese
- 50ml double cream
- Toasted coconut flakes, to decorate

EXTRA EQUIPMENT

You will need six 100ml dessert glasses, a food processor, a large bowl, a piping bag and a large round-tip nozzle.

METHOD

Firstly, put the two tins of coconut milk into the freezer and leave them there until required.

Add the digestive biscuits into a food processor and blitz them until they resemble fine crumbs. Mix through the desiccated coconut, then add the melted butter and blitz again until all the mixture is coated.

Add a tablespoon of the biscuit mixture into each glass and press it down. Set aside.

For the cheesecake mixture, take the coconut milk out of the freezer and open the tins, scooping out the solid coconut cream that sits on top. Put the solid coconut cream and cream cheese into a large bowl and whisk together until smooth. Add the double cream and mix it through.

Fill a piping bag, fitted with a large round-tip nozzle, with the cream cheese mixture and pipe it evenly into each glass, on top of the biscuit base.

Leave the cheesecake to set for 1 hour in the fridge before serving with a sprinkle of toasted coconut to decorate.

DRINKS

☙ WATERMELON ICED TEA ☙

It's hot and you need to rehydrate. If you're bored of having water all the time,
try something different with this thirst-quenching iced tea.
This recipe requires some patience but it's well worth the wait.

Serves: 4 ☙ Time: 15 minutes, plus 2 hours 30 minutes' cooling time ☙
Difficulty rating: ♩

INGREDIENTS

* 6 black teabags
* 1 litre boiling water
* 1 small watermelon, sliced in half
* 3 sprigs fresh mint, plus extra for serving
* Juice of 3 limes
* 1 lime, sliced

EXTRA EQUIPMENT

You will need a blender and a large heatproof jug.

METHOD

Place the teabags in a large heatproof jug then carefully pour the boiling water over them.

Allow them to steep for about 5–10 minutes then remove the teabags and let the tea cool down to room temperature.

Once cooled, place in the fridge and chill for at least 1 hour.

Scoop out the flesh of one half of the watermelon and remove as many seeds as possible. Place the flesh into a blender and blitz until completely juiced. Cut the other half into slices for serving.

Pour the watermelon juice through a sieve into a large bowl using a spoon to help pass it all through. Throw away the remaining pulp then add the mint leaves to the watermelon juice and chill it in the fridge for 1 hour.

When you're ready to make the iced tea, mix the watermelon juice into the chilled tea, remove the mint leaves from the mixture then squeeze in the fresh lime juice and stir it all through.

Serve with lots of ice in tall glasses and garnish with a few lime slices, fresh mint leaves and a slice of watermelon.

Any leftover tea should be covered and kept in the fridge for up to 4 days. The watermelon juice and tea will separate if left, so always stir it thoroughly before serving.

🍍 FLAMINGO FLOCKTAIL 🍍

Gather your flock of best friends and serve this refreshing summer mocktail which is sure to get the party started.

Serves: 4 🍍 Time: 15 minutes 🍍 Difficulty rating: 🦩

INGREDIENTS

* 500ml pink grapefruit juice
* 300ml pink lemonade
* Juice of 2 limes, plus extra for the decoration
* Ice
* 2 tbsp granulated sugar
* 4 segments of pink grapefruit

EXTRA EQUIPMENT

You will need a large jug and four cocktail glasses.

METHOD

Add all the ingredients except the sugar into a large jug filled with ice and stir it all together to combine.

Pour the sugar on to a plate then wet the rim of the cocktail glasses with lime juice and dip them into the plate of sugar.

Pour the mocktail mixture into cocktail glasses and serve with a segment of pink grapefruit.

🍍 MONKEY MILKSHAKE 🍍

Who said a bit of monkeying around was a bad thing? Shake things up with this decadent dessert drink – you'll be swinging from the ceiling with all that sugar inside you.

Serves: 2 🍍 **Time: 15 minutes** 🍍 **Difficulty rating:** 🦩

INGREDIENTS

* 6 scoops vanilla ice cream
* 2 bananas, peeled
* 100ml semi-skimmed milk
* 4 tbsp cocoa powder
* 1 tsp vanilla extract
* Whipped cream, to decorate
* Grated chocolate, to decorate
* Banana chips, to decorate (optional)

EXTRA EQUIPMENT

You will need a blender and two milkshake glasses.

METHOD

Put the ice cream, bananas, milk, cocoa powder and vanilla extract into a blender and blitz them together until smooth.

Pour equally between two glasses, then top with whipped cream, grated chocolate and a banana chip per drink.

PINEAPPLE PUNCH

Pack a pineapple punch and delight your guests with this super-satisfying mocktail.

Serves: 2　　Time: 15 minutes　　Difficulty rating:

INGREDIENTS

* A few cubes of ice
* 100g frozen pineapple chunks
* 200ml pineapple juice
* 200ml coconut milk
* 2 pineapple wedges, to garnish
* 4 cocktail cherries, to garnish

EXTRA EQUIPMENT

You will need a blender.

METHOD

Put the ice and frozen pineapple into a blender and blitz together until a paste is formed.

Add the pineapple juice and the coconut milk then blend all together until fully combined and smooth.

Serve into your glasses of choice then add a pineapple wedge and two cocktail cherries per glass to garnish.

🍍 TOUCAN SUNRISE 🍍

Rise and shine with this delicious alternative to your morning orange juice.

Serves: 2 🍍 Time: 5 minutes 🍍 Difficulty rating: 🦩

INGREDIENTS

* 300ml orange juice
* 100ml mango purée
* Ice
* 4 tbsp grenadine
* 2 slices of fresh orange, to garnish
* 4 cocktail cherries, to garnish

EXTRA EQUIPMENT

You will need a large jug and two cocktail glasses.

METHOD

Pour the orange juice and mango purée into a large jug and stir them together to combine.

Fill two cocktail glasses with ice and pour the orange and mango mixture over the top.

Carefully pour 2 tbsp of grenadine over the top of each cocktail and allow it to settle at the bottom.

To garnish, add a slice of fresh orange and a couple of cocktail cherries on a stick.

INDEX